the little GREEN BOOK of Shopping

For Mum and Dad, loving parents and shrewd shoppers

THIS IS A CARLTON BOOK

Text, illustrations and design copyright © 2008
Carlton Books Limited

This edition published by
Carlton Books Limited 2008
20 Mortimer Street
London W1T 3JW

A CIP catalogue record for this book is available from
the British Library.

ISBN 978-1-84732-071-1

Printed and bound in Singapore

Senior Executive Editor: Lisa Dyer
Senior Art Editor: Gulen Shevki-Taylor
Designer: Emma Wicks
Production: Kate Pimm

Your **Carbon Footprint** is the amount of carbon dioxide emitted
due to your daily activities – from washing a load of laundry to
driving to work. See www.carbonfootprint.com for ways to reduce
your impact on the environment.

DIANE MILLIS

the little GREEN BOOK of Shopping

250 TIPS FOR AN ECO LIFESTYLE

CARLTON
BOOKS

The everyday choices you face as a consumer can have a huge impact on the environment. Whether you are buying food at your local supermarket or considering big purchases like a new car or house, this book will help you make informed and responsible decisions that enable you to live in a more sustainable way.

1 DO LESS SHOPPING

One of the most beneficial things you can do for the environment is shop less. Just 20% of the world's population is consuming more than 80% of the earth's natural resources due to our insatiable demand for products, be it cheap fashion, new foods or groovy gadgets. Start by observing 'Buy Nothing Day', an annual event celebrated in more than 40 countries worldwide. For more information, see www.adbusters.org (for North America) or www.buynothingday.co.uk (UK) for dates.

REUSE AND RECYCLE WHAT YOU DO BUY

Make sure you get the most out of your money and the resources used to make a product by doing your utmost to reuse or recycle it. From using yogurt pots for planting seeds to joining an online recycling service like Freecycle or eFreeko, there's more to this than a weekly trip to the bottle bank.

3

MAKE DO AND MEND

Before you throw something away because it is old, stained or broken, try to repair it. Old furniture can be reupholstered or revarnished, while clothing can be taken to a tailor's and repaired. After a couple of months, you'll find it becomes a habit to fix rather than discard.

4 GO ORGANIC

By buying certified-organic products you will be supporting a farming system that is better for wildlife, uses less harmful pesticides and produces less CO_2.

5 LOOK FOR FAIRTRADE

Look out for products that have been certified by FLO-CERT, which will carry the fairtrade mark. The organization guarantees that disadvantaged producers in the developing world are getting a better deal by receiving a minimum price that covers the cost of sustainable production, as well as an extra premium that is invested in social or economic development projects.

6 KEEP IT LOCAL

Buying products flown in or transported halfway around the country via distribution centres will do nothing to help you reduce your carbon footprint. Ideally, buy directly from local producers. In the UK, some food retailers are labelling products that have been imported by air with a small aeroplane symbol and the words 'air freighted'.

7 LIMIT 'MADE IN CHINA' ITEMS

The 'made in China' logo can be seen just about everywhere, but demand from western countries plays a big part in the expansion of the Chinese economy, which is a big user of fossil-fuel intensive energy and is highly polluting.

8 WATCH OUT FOR LUXURY ITEMS

Celebrity-endorsed luxury brands haven't scored well in a World Wildlife Fund UK investigation into their eco-friendliness. Its report, *Deeper Luxury,* claims luxury brands have been slow to recognize their responsibilities to the environment and the charity is now launching a 'Star Charter' for celebrities to adopt, which commits them to considering the environmental and social performance of the brands they endorse.

9 BE WARY OF ECO 'JUNK'

Being green is about saving the planet, not your status. Don't fall into the trap of buying goods that are labelled as 'eco' or 'fairtrade' just because they are 'worthy'. Whereas many of these products are perfectly legitimate, you may not actually need them and the best thing you can do for the planet is not to buy things you don't need in the first place. Find ways of reusing what you do have or trading with someone else instead.

10 IMPORT MADNESS

Globalization has led to some bizarre figures for international trade. According to the 2007 New Economics Foundation report *Chinadependence*, the UK sent 21 tonnes of mineral water all the way to Australia and brought 20 tonnes back in 2006; and the amount of beer the UK sold in Spain is almost the same as the amount Spain sold in the UK. The environmental cost of these import/exports is very high, so do your part and avoid buying imports.

11 IT'S NOT ALWAYS SIMPLE

Many shopping decisions are complicated. For example, research has shown that the emissions produced by growing flowers in Kenya and flying them to the UK can be less than a fifth of the emissions that come from flowers grown in Dutch greenhouses. Plus, what can be good from a green perspective could be bad from an ethical one. British shoppers spend over £1 million a day on imported fruit and vegetables from Africa, and the livelihoods of more than a million farmers and their families depend on this trade. Do as much research as you can.

12 SHIPPING DOWNSIDE

You may think buying a product that has arrived on your shores by boat is a green option, but think again. According to Friends of the Earth, diesel-powered ocean-going ships burn some of the dirtiest fuel on the planet today and research has shown that the number of people dying from heart and lung disease as a result of under-regulated shipping emissions is estimated to grow by 40% by 2012.

13 A ROAD LESS TRAVELLED

Walk or cycle to the shops – driving 10.5 km (6 ½ miles) to buy your shopping emits more carbon than flying a pack of Kenyan green beans to London. If you absolutely have to drive, make sure you make fewer trips by buying in bulk when you get there and look into sharing your shopping trips and car with neighbours.

14 BUY ETHICAL

Millions of people around the world are working in hazardous conditions for a wage that barely meets their basic needs. Make sure the products you buy have not been made at others' expense by checking the ethical policies of the manufacturers and retailers (ideally, they will be members of the Ethical Trading Initiative). For help, look at Ethical Consumer's online guide – Ethiscore (www.ethiscore.org). It rates companies against 18 environmental, animal welfare and human rights issues.

15 SELECT SUSTAINABLE

Get to know the certification schemes for sustainable production, such as Forest Stewardship Council (FSC) certification for wood from sustainable forests, and Marine Stewardship Council (MSC) for fish from fisheries that are well managed and sustainable. The Rainforest Alliance also certifies sustainable agriculture, tourism and forestry (www.rainforest-alliance.org).

16 AVOID PETRO-CHEMICALS

From mineral oil in beauty products, to solvents in paints and detergents in washing powder, petro-chemicals are present in many of the things we buy. But the clue is in the name – they are derived from petroleum, which is itself derived from fossil fuels. Read the label before you buy and try to avoid these products.

17 BE LABEL-WISE

You can't be a truly green shopper until you've mastered the art of labelling. Products that claim to be 'natural' and 'pure' could be no more so than any other – these terms do not have to be proven. Many ingredients do not have to be listed – the ingredient 'parfum' (fragrance), for example, can be used to describe up to 100 different chemicals. Arm yourself with as much information as you can and always read the label!

18 WRITE A LIST

It's incredibly simple – but it works! To avoid too many impulse purchases, pin a shopping list up in your kitchen and you can update it as you run out of things. Then take it to the store and stick to it. If you still find it hard to fight temptation, then consider buying your groceries online where you can be systematic about your shopping.

19 ARMCHAIR SHOPPING

The internet offers the chance to reduce the impact of your shopping by buying secondhand goods (through online charities or eBay, for example) or by sourcing goods from ethical and fairtrade sources. One such site is www.onevillage.com, which supports artisans' cooperatives and sells hand-made, sustainable products from partner enterprises that strive to build up communities' quality of life.

20 BRING YOUR OWN BAGS

We use over 1.2 trillion plastic bags a year – an average of about 300 bags for each adult on the planet – but only for an average of 12 minutes before throwing them away. The damage goes beyond visual pollution – plastic bags in landfill sites take up to 500 years to decompose, while those that end up in our oceans kill at least 100,000 birds, whales, seals and turtles every year.

21 CHOOSE A STURDY SHOPPER

Rather than using the plastic or paper bags supplied by your supermarket, invest in a few shopping bags made from renewable materials such as jute, linen, hemp and cotton. Make sure they are sturdy so they last for years, and keep them handy by the door or in your car so you never forget them when you go shopping.

22 PLAGUED BY PLASTIC

The world's annual consumption of plastic materials has increased from around 5 million tonnes in the 1950s to nearly 100 million tonnes today. Plastics may be cheap, but they cause pollution at all stages of their production and use, with some forms of plastics, such as vinyl, constantly giving off harmful gases. If you must buy plastic make sure you do what you can to recycle it.

23 OPT FOR LESS PACKAGING

We all wade through mountains of packaging to get to the things we actually want and it's getting worse – in the UK packaging increased by 12% between 1999 and 2005 and the US generates around 135 kg (300 lb) of packaging waste per person each year. Choose the least-packaged items possible; you are also entitled to leave any unnecessary packaging with a retailer so that they get the message.

24 BUY RECYCLED

Buying products made from recycled materials instead of products made from new materials saves natural resources and reduces greenhouse gases. This doesn't just mean recycling your own goods – make sure you buy recycled products as well.

25 THE BEST YOU CAN AFFORD

The better quality an item is, the longer it is likely to last. If you are a 'buy cheap, buy twice' kind of person, you are likely to be throwing things away far more than is good for the planet – and your wallet.

26 SEEK OUT ENERGY-EFFICIENT PRODUCTS

Many electrical products now come with an energy rating – the EnergyGuide and Energy Star labels in the US, for example. Check any product you are about to purchase and make sure it has the highest possible rating.

27 REMEMBER THE FOUR RS

Few products seem to be built to last and many of us don't know how to carry out basic repairs but before buying you should check whether a product is rechargeable, repairable, refillable or reusable.

28 CHEMICAL COCKTAILS

More than 300 man-made chemicals have been found in human bodies; unsurprising perhaps given they are everywhere – in our food, beauty products, sofas, carpets and washing powders. There is growing evidence that links some of these chemicals to birth defects, cancer and other diseases. Minimize your exposure by buying chemical-light products.

29 CAN YOU RECYCLE IT?

Whenever you buy something, you are taking responsibility for its impact on the planet from then on. Make sure it can be recycled – look out for a recycling logo and find local recycling services. For electrical items such as fridges and freezers, check with the manufacturer who made it or the retailer who sold it – they have a responsibility to provide assistance with recycling.

30 NO NEED FOR NEW

Vintage clothes, second-hand books and videos … charity shops, thrift stores, car boot (garage) sales and the church jumble sale are still great places for green shoppers. Many charities have also branched out into offering online shopping options, too.

BUY LOCAL AND SMALL

Independent local shops and street markets are probably the greenest grocers. A recent study has shown that big supermarkets emit on average three times as much CO_2 per square foot than the average independent grocer, while a separate study has found that a higher proportion of packaging from street markets was recyclable than that found in the big supermarket chains.

32 SINGLE-USE IS A WASTE

Energy is used to make and distribute single-use products such as disposable cameras and barbecues. You use them just the once and then energy is used to transport them to a landfill where they could take hundreds of years to decompose, leaching toxins as they do.

33 BEWARE BIOFUELS

Biofuels, particularly ethanol and diesel made from plants such as corn, sugarcane and rapeseed, may not be the easy answer. Although they offer a way of reducing greenhouse gas emissions, they are also a real threat to biodiversity. To keep up with demand, huge areas of land could be planted with these crops, which would involve the loss of wildlife-rich landscapes. There is also a chance that switching to these crops could lead to food shortages.

34 PROBLEMS WITH PALM OIL

Palm oil is found in one in ten supermarket products including chocolate, bread, detergents and lipsticks. But palm oil plantations are the most significant cause of rainforest loss in Malaysia and Indonesia – palm oil plantations were responsible for 87% of deforestation in Malaysia between 1985 and 2000 and the industry could drive the orangutan to extinction. Check whether palm oil is present – it could be lurking under the generic label 'vegetable oil'.

35 QUIT SMOKING

You know it makes sense to quit for your health, but did you know it will help more than the air around you? It could also help the environment – each year, 200,000 hectares (50,000 acres) of woodland are destroyed in order to clear the way for tobacco plantations.

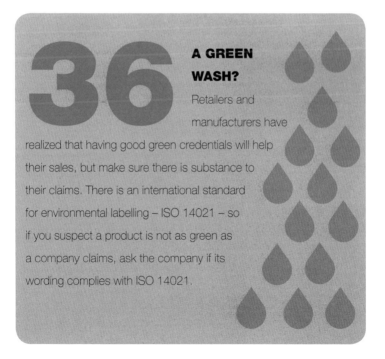

36 A GREEN WASH?

Retailers and manufacturers have realized that having good green credentials will help their sales, but make sure there is substance to their claims. There is an international standard for environmental labelling – ISO 14021 – so if you suspect a product is not as green as a company claims, ask the company if its wording complies with ISO 14021.

37 GET SYMBOL SAVVY

There are few internationally recognized 'green' symbols such as the EU's Ecolabel flower or the star logo for US Energy Star. But new ones are cropping up all the time – such as the new Future Friendly logo, which is an initiative of multinational giant Proctor & Gamble. Many of these symbol schemes have not been independently verified as being truly green so check with trusted sources such as the Ethical Consumer Research Association.

38 PUMP SPRAY IS BEST

While they no longer contain ozone-depleting chlorofluorocarbons (CFCs), aerosol cans do contain other propellants that contribute to global warming, and minute particles of the propellant contaminate the air you breathe. An alternative is hand-pump spray bottles, which are refillable.

39 TREAT CLAIMS WITH CARE

A new generation of degradeable, biodegradeable and compostable packaging is hitting the store shelves but they may not be the answer to all our packaging woes. Compostable packaging will often only break down at temperatures higher than the average home compost. If they are not disposed of correctly they could end up in landfills where they will increase the amounts of methane gases generated.

40 BUY RECYCLED PAPER

Whether it's toilet paper or office paper, recycling one tonne of paper saves 15 average-sized trees and 28–70% less energy is used to produce recycled rather than virgin paper. On top of this, the paper would otherwise end up on landfill sites where it biodegrades to produce methane gas – a potent greenhouse gas and contributor to global warming.

41 PVC – THE HARD FACTS

It can be found in wallpaper, shower curtains and other plastics around the home, but polyvinyl chloride (PVC) contains chemicals including phthalates that have been linked to cancer and reproductive health problems. Also, when produced or burned PVC plastic releases dioxins, which can cause cancer and harm the immune and reproductive systems.

42 TOXIC FIRE RETARDANTS

Polybrominated diphenyl ethers (PBDEs) are used as a flame retardant in many everyday products, including furniture, mattresses, computers, TV sets and cars – and they are now found in people, animals and the environment. The levels of PBDEs in women's breast milk have been doubling every five years, with the exception of Sweden where PBDEs have been banned since the 1990s. The EU has banned the most toxic forms of PBDEs, but in the US only a few states have gone ahead with bans.

43 SUSTAINABLE PROPERTY

Look for a property that already has good green credentials – well insulated and double-glazed for starters. In the UK, there is a voluntary standard for new housing – the Code for Sustainable Homes. The government expects all new homes to be carbon neutral by 2016 but at present only 2% of new private homes meet minimum standards. In the US, the Leadership in Energy and Environmental Design (LEED) is the nationally accepted benchmark for the design, construction and operation of green buildings.

44 A SUSTAINABLE LOCATION

When shopping for your next home, take a look at the sustainability of the town or city in which it's located. Some have become plastic-bag free, for example, or might have ambitious plans for cycle networks or green spaces. Or you could be a pioneer and take up residence in one of the world's eco-towns or cities – ten are planned for the UK, while others are to be built in China and Abu Dhabi.

45 BUY FROM A GREEN AGENT

To help narrow down your search for a carbon-light home, consider using specialist real estate agents. Examples include GreenMoves, an 'eco property for sale' website for the UK market, and the GreenHomesForSale site for properties in the US.

46 BE A GREEN BORROWER

Make sure your home loan benefits the environment by getting a green mortgage. The lender will either plant a certain number of trees per loan to offset its carbon footprint or will donate cash to environmental projects on your behalf. Some green mortgage providers will only lend on properties that provide 'an ecological payback', such as new homes built with recycled or sustainable materials, or homes that will be made as energy efficient as possible.

47

THE POWER OF GREEN

Rather than use non-renewable sources of power – coal, oil and natural gas – go for green power instead. Many electricity companies now offer power from renewable sources such as solar, hydro or wind. It might cost more but it will cost the planet less.

48

TAKE A WIND CHECK

Putting a turbine on your roof may not be the best renewable energy option for your home. It is unlikely to get sufficiently strong and consistent winds at roof height, especially as most houses are built in sheltered areas, and the vibrations might actually damage your home. Check with an experienced advisor before going ahead.

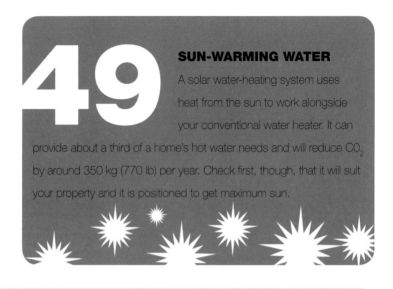

49 SUN-WARMING WATER

A solar water-heating system uses heat from the sun to work alongside your conventional water heater. It can provide about a third of a home's hot water needs and will reduce CO_2 by around 350 kg (770 lb) per year. Check first, though, that it will suit your property and it is positioned to get maximum sun.

50 LET THE SUN SHINE IN

In areas where there is plenty of daylight, it may be worth installing solar photovoltaic panels on your roof to convert light energy into electric energy. They are unlikely to meet all your power needs but you should be able to cut your power use and costs. Check for any government grants that might make it less expensive and find out about options for selling the energy generated back to your energy supplier.

51 COOKING WITH WOOD

As long as the wood used comes from a sustainable source, using wood as a fuel will not cause a net increase of CO_2 in the atmosphere. It also produces less acid rain chemicals than any fossil fuel and, if burned efficiently, will release minimal amounts of soot, hydrocarbons or other pollutants. Choices include: a wood stove, which will usually heat one room but could have a back boiler to heat water, a central heating wood boiler, wood pellet stoves and boilers that use wood industry waste, and wood-chip boilers for larger houses.

52 BUY A LOGMAKER

For free fuel, make your own logs from old newspapers using a logmaker. Just soak the paper and place in the mould, squeeze and after drying the log will burn as well as wood for up to an hour in a woodburning stove.

53

INVEST IN A HEAT PUMP

Heat pumps transfer heat from the ground (geo-thermal), air or water into a building to provide heating and, in some cases, to pre-heat hot water. They can also be reversed to cool a house in the summer. A geo-thermal heat pump will save 2–8 tonnes of CO_2 per year, depending on the type of fuel being replaced.

54

THE POWER OF WATER

If you're lucky enough to have a stream or river running through your garden, consider buying a hydropower system. The output will depend on the flow rate of the waterway but the energy generated will avoid the use of fossil fuels, help cut CO_2 emissions and save on your electricity bills. Start small with a battery-charging micro-hydro system, which costs about the same as a good-quality washing machine.

55 SEAL THE GAPS

If there's one thing you should buy for your home, it's insulation. Draught excluders for doors and windows, loft insulation, cavity wall insulation, under-floor insulation – there are plenty of areas you need to consider. Around half of the heat lost in a typical home disappears through the walls and loft so they should be first on the list. Choose sustainable materials such as sheep's wool or cellulose fibre made from recycled fire-proofed newsprint.

56 MEASURE YOUR ENERGY

An energy-saving meter will help you monitor the amount of electricity you are using around the home and should ultimately make it easier for you to cut back. A sensor and transmitter is attached to your meter and updates a remote monitor every six seconds. You can install it and can see how much power you're using, when you switch on the television, for example.

57 CONDENSING BOILER IS BEST

If the 4 million old, inefficient boilers in UK homes were replaced it would save 2.5 million tonnes of CO_2 each year by 2010. Choose a high-efficiency condensing boiler – it's the most efficient and should reduce your heating bill by around 30%. In the US there is a tax rebate for the installation of condensing boilers. Remember to buy an insulating jacket for your boiler and insulate pipes at the same time to lessen heat loss.

58 RESIST THE AIR CONDITIONER

With hotter summers predicted the demand for air conditioners is also likely to rise – already around two-thirds of all homes in the US have them – but they can double the electricity consumption of a house. In the US, air conditioning accounts for 16% of the average household's electricity consumption – the same as all lighting, music systems, televisons, video and DVD players, desktop computers and printers combined. There are other ways to cool your home, such as drawing curtains, improving ventilation, installing loft insulation or even building a green roof on your home.

OPT FOR CFLS OR LEDS

A house has on average 23 light bulbs, which could all be replaced by energy-saving compact fluorescent light bulbs (CFLs). These use only a fifth to a quarter of the electricity of ordinary bulbs and last up to ten times longer. Even better, opt for light emitting diodes (LEDs), which use even less energy than CFLs and can last up to ten times longer (and 130 times longer than conventional incandescent bulbs).

BUY DOUBLE-GLAZING

Stop your heat flying out the window by installing double-glazing, ideally using low emissivity (Low-E) glass. Double-glazing cuts heat loss through windows by 50%. If this is too costly, then at least invest in some plastic insulating film and stick a layer over each pane – it will achieve a similar effect for a fraction of the price and if applied correctly won't show.

61 CHOOSE HEAVY CURTAINS

When you next consider buying new curtains, choose thick ones, which can be as effective at keeping in warmth as an extra layer of glazing – particularly if they have thick thermal linings. Unlined curtains cut heat loss through windows by a third; insulated curtains reduce it by half.

62 PICK ECO-FRIENDLY WALLPAPER

Look out for greener wallpapers – they should use chlorine-free paper sourced from sustainably managed forests, be printed using water-based inks, which have less impact on the environment and contain no hazardous solvents. Check also whether the manufacturer recycles its waste from edge trimmings and look out for paste made from natural materials and free from fungicides, preservatives and synthetic resins.

63

LOW VOC PAINTS

Decorators have a 40% increased risk of developing lung cancer due to the toxic effect of chemicals in paints, such as volatile organic compounds (VOCs), biocides, fungicides and solvents. Make sure the paints you use are as natural as possible, and contain none of these chemical hazards.

64

LOOK INTO SPECIALITY ECO PAINTS

Some natural paint manufacturers have developed paints that absorb pollutants such as formaldehyde, solvents and VOCs given off by synthetic furnishings. Wall-insulating paints are also available which help to regulate the temperature inside throughout the year.

65 TRY WATER-BASED PAINT STRIPPERS

Conventional paint strippers contain solvents that carry health risks, such as dichloromethane – a highly toxic carcinogen. Instead, buy a water-based stripper that is solvent-free and will biodegrade. It does not dry out quickly, enabling you to strip a large area in one go, and will wash off with water.

66 NATURAL WALL COVERS

Rather than painting your walls, consider lining them with natural materials from renewable sources such as bamboo, jute, sisal, seagrass and even recycled paper. They help to absorb more noise than uncovered walls and also act as extra insulation.

67 BUY A GOOD QUALITY DOORMAT

A typical household carpet will be harbouring a selection of particularly nasty chemicals carried into a house on the soles of shoes. A US Environmental Protection Agency study has found that domestic pesticide levels are increased up to 400-fold by contamination trodden in on the feet of people and pets. By using a good quality doormat, and taking shoes off at the door, you should be able to reduce the toxicity of your carpets.

68 CARE WITH CARPETS

Avoid synthetic carpets made from nylon and polyester – they are less durable, often use dyes derived from petrochemicals and may be pre-treated with fire retardants. Opt for natural carpets made from wool, linen or cotton but be aware that wool can sometimes be contaminated with pesticides or treated with stain-proofing chemicals. The backing material should also be natural – hessian, hemp, cotton or jute rather than polyurethane or latex foam, or PVC underlays, which can emit VOCs.

69

LINO INSTEAD OF VINYL

Vinyl flooring is made from PVC combined with fungicides, pigments and plasticizers. Opt for lino as an alternative. It is a natural floor covering made from linseed oil and other natural and renewable ingredients such as cork and wood flour. Lino is one of the most sustainable flooring materials available; it has a life-span of 30-40 years, is naturally anti-bacterial and will biodegrade at the end of its life.

70

PUT A CORK IT

With its many environmental and social benefits, cork is a renewable and sustainable resource. But check that the cork tiles you pick have not been sealed with PVC or polyurethane, neither of which are desirable chemicals to have in the home. Instead, source unsealed cork flooring and seal it yourself with low-VOC varnish.

71 FEEL THE WOOD BENEATH YOUR FEET

A hardwood floor from reclaimed sources not only looks great but it also can be a good environmental choice. If you can't get reclaimed wood, the next best thing is wood that has come from sustainable sources and is Forest Stewardship Council (FSC) certified.

72 TREAT WOOD NATURALLY

Invest in some natural finishes for your wooden floors (and other woods in your home). These include jojoba oil, linseed oil and tung oil from the nut of the tung tree that grows naturally in regions of China. But be sure to get 100% pure oil —many modern linseed and tung products are cut with solvents and other chemicals.

73 BUY ORGANIC COTTON

If buying cotton soft furnishings, bedding, towels or clothing, always buy organic. Cotton farming uses one quarter of the world's pesticides and the number of cotton farmers suffering acute pesticide poisoning each year is between 25 and 77 million worldwide, according to a report by the Environmental Justice Foundation (EJF) and the Pesticide Action Network.

74 BED DOWN ON AN ORGANIC MATTRESS

Certified organic mattresses made from natural fibres like cotton, wool and hemp provide comfort and reduce carbon emissions and pollution created during the manufacturing process. You also won't be exposed to the chemical residues that can cause allergies. Look out also for other natural mattresses made with latex, coir, horsehair and camel hair.

75 SLEEP ON A FUTON

Save on the wood or metal needed to make a bed frame by sleeping on a futon mattress, which is designed to be placed directly on the floor or on a woven rush mat. Look for futons made with organic and unbleached cotton and wool.

76 NATURAL BEDLINEN

There is evidence that the fire retardants, moth repellents, easy care and anti-pilling finishes which are routinely applied to bed linen may contribute to childhood asthma, eczema and even cot death. Explore natural alternatives such as hemp and organic unbleached cotton – virtually all polycotton, all 'easy-care', 'crease-resistant', and 'permanent-press' cottons are treated with formaldehyde.

77 FIGHT THE MITES

Neem oil is a natural insecticide and spraying it on to your mattress and bedding could help prevent dust mite colonization. It is derived from the seed of the Neem tree and is an entirely natural product. Either dilute some neem oil with water and use a spray dispenser or buy a ready-made neem oil spray.

78 REST YOUR HEAD ON BUCKWHEAT

Try using a buckwheat pillow that has been filled with certified organic, unfumigated buckwheat hulls and covered with organic cotton. You can remove or add hulls to adjust the pillow to suit you.

79 BUY BAMBOO TOWELS

You can buy towels that are made from 70% bamboo fibre and 30% cotton. Bamboo grows extremely quickly and doesn't need any pesticides. Bamboo towels are three times as absorbent as cotton, and should be laundered at 40°C before first using them as they have not been subjected to any wet processes such as scouring, bleaching or dyeing after weaving.

80 GO DIGITAL

Save on film and processing chemicals by investing in a digital camera. By picking the shots you like you'll reduce the waste that comes from printing an entire roll of film. Just be sure to print on the most eco-friendly paper you can find. And, while you're at it, invest in an MP3 player and give up your CD habit – they're bad for the environment.

81 AN ELECTRONIC TAKE OVER

By 2010, the consumer electronics sector will be the biggest single user of domestic electricity, overtaking kitchen appliances and lighting, and by 2020, entertainment, computers and gadgets will account for 45% of electricity used in our homes. In the UK alone, it will take the equivalent of 14 average-sized power stations just to run them! So choose and use your electronics carefully.

82 SAY GOODBYE TO STANDBY

The average household has up to 12 gadgets left on standby or charging at any one time, with the television left on standby for up to 17.5 hours a day. Look out for products without a standby function or those which have been designed to use less power on standby. There are also products available that connect all your appliances and let you turn them all off at the socket with one click, including one which turns off PC peripherals (printers, monitors and so on) when you turn off your computer.

83 GO DIGITAL

Instead of listening to the radio through your TV, invest in a digital radio. You consume 10 to 20 times more power using using your TV to listen to your tunes rather than through a digital radio.

84 CLOCKWORK MUSIC

Buy a wind-up radio to save energy. They come in several different styles, including ones with solar panels to help charge the batteries. There's even a digital-multi-band solar/wind-up radio complete with built-in clock/alarm.

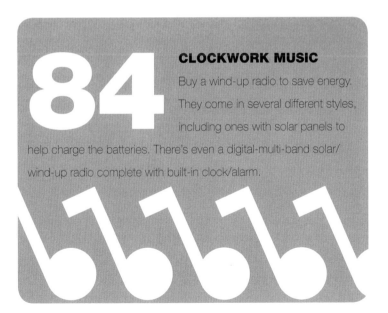

THE POWER OF WATER

You can now buy digital alarm clocks and calculators that run on water-powered batteries. To keep the battery going, refill it as the water evaporates, typically every two to three months. The battery will last a minimum of two years and all the components of the H_2O battery are recyclable.

RECHARGE YOUR BATTERIES

Conventional batteries contain cadmium and mercury and must be treated as hazardous waste. The UK generates 20,000-30,000 tonnes of waste general-purpose batteries every year, with less than 1,000 tonnes being recycled. Three billion household dry cell batteries are sold and discarded in the United States each year, producing more than 125,000 tonnes of waste. Rechargeable batteries last longer, cost less to use and help keep toxins out of the waste stream.

87 INVEST IN A SOLAR CHARGER

You can buy solar chargers that let you recharge your iPod, phone, camera or other mobile device virtually anywhere if you position the solar panels in direct sunlight. A full charger delivers enough charge to extend your play time up to 9 hours, or fully charge your iPod with enough power left over to top up your mobile phone.

88 SMALL-SCREEN ENTERTAINMENT

There are real concerns that the new wave of hi-tech televisions will increase CO_2 emissions because flat screen televisions that are larger than 60 cm (24 in) use over three times the electricity of their conventional counterparts. Liquid crystal display (LCD) screens consume the least electricity and also contain less lead than the cathode ray tubes (CRTs) used in electronic televisions, but you should choose the smallest screen you can.

89 BUY UPGRADEABLE COMPUTERS

Avoid operating systems and software that cannot be upgraded electronically – such as cheap factory sealed computers that are designed to be thrown away once no longer needed. Two million working Pentium PCs end up in landfill sites in the UK every year and only 20% of all discarded UK computers are recycled. When buying a new computer ask for readily upgradable hardware, make sure spare parts and service will be available, and check to see that memory is easily expandable.

90 E-WASTE DANGERS

Greenpeace is campaigning against the dangerous growth of electronic scrap (e-waste) containing toxic chemicals and heavy metals that cannot be disposed of or recycled safely and that often ends up being illegally dumped in developing countries. Check its Green Electronics Guide, which rates the major electronics makers.

91 RETURN TO MAKER

Try to buy from a manufacturer who is prepared to take your old computer back for disposal, whether it is their brand or not. You will be supporting a more responsible approach to e-waste.

92 WOOD WORK

Have a break from plastic and opt for a more natural look – a Swedish company (www.swedx.se) now sells computer monitors and keyboards in wooden cases and even a mouse made of ash, which can be recycled. Online, you can also buy bamboo casings for your computer screen, keyboard and mouse.

93 LOW-ENERGY LAPTOPS

Laptops consume one-eighth of the power of desktop computers because mobile processors are designed for long battery life, which means they are state of the art in terms of power management. Laptops also use the bare minimum of components in order to keep their size and weight down, so there will be less waste when it is no longer needed.

94 GO BACK TO AN INKJET PRINTER

Inkjet printers use up to 90% less energy than a laser printer. To save on power and paper, check also that your printer can shrink your document to fit two, four or more pages on a single sheet and that it can handle double-sided printing.

95

RECYCLE PRINT CARTRIDGES

Over 700 million ink cartridges were thrown away worldwide in 2003 – and they are all non-biodegradable. Cut your environmental impact by buying remanufactured cartridges and recycling old ones.

96

PAPER FOR PRINTING

Buy recycled paper for your printer and be sure to recycle it after use. Did you know that recycling 1 tonne of printing or copier paper saves more than 2 tonnes of wood? But do remember to avoid printing in the first place – 115 billion sheets of paper are used annually for personal computers and the average daily web user prints 28 pages daily. Given that an estimated 95% of business information is still stored on paper, there is still a long way to go.

97 SWITCH SERVICE PROVIDERS

A growing number of internet service providers are now operating energy-saving business practices such as encouraging staff to use public transport. Some use solar-power in their offices while others offset their carbon emissions so check them out.

98 HOLD ONTO YOUR MOBILE

There are more than 7 billion mobile (cell) phones in the world and only 1.3 billion users. On top of that the average user replaces their handset every 18 months and over 100 million mobiles are thrown away each year. Mobiles that end up in landfill leak several contaminants such as lead, brominated flame retardants and cadmium. Instead of upgrading every year, hold onto your phone for as long as possible and recycle it when you no longer want it – there are many charities that offer this service. Look out too for phones with biodegradeable covers that are already available in Japan.

99 A NEW NETWORK CAN WORK

Not all mobile (cell phone) service providers are equal in green terms.

Look for the greenest possible, such as Green Mobile in the UK (www.greenmobile.co.uk), which asks its customers to hold on to their existing handset for one more year and in return gives a rebate and donation to the one of its two partner charities: the Woodland Trust or Friends of the Earth.

100 BUY RECLAIMED

You will not only feel virtuous for doing your bit to support the recycling of products, but will also have a unique and often amazing piece of furniture. Go to salvage yards or buy from companies that specialize in selling reclaimed items or re-using them to make new products. Items to look out for are those from schools, libraries, hospitals or churches such as seats, doors, worktops, tiles, bricks, sinks, free-standing baths and fireplaces.

CHECK IT'S CERTIFIED

101 If you are buying wooden furniture make sure it comes from a sustainable source – and the easiest way to be sure is to check if it carries the Forest Stewardship Council (FSC) logo or is certified by the umbrella organization, the Rainforest Alliance.

AWAY FROM THE NORM

102 There are plenty of recycled furniture options out there, including tables and seating made from washing machine drums, recycled cardboard and recycled plastic, or even reclaimed cinema chairs. Be different and buy something unexpected and possibly unique.

103 WELL UPHOLSTERED

Avoid upholstery that uses synthetic foams, foam rubber, latex or plastic coverings, because these emit VOCs (volatile organic compounds). Cotton is one of the most pesticide-ridden crops and leather uses hazardous chemicals in its processing, so look for the most natural coverings possible – such as those made from organic cotton, hemp and linen.

104 SUPPORT CRAFTSMEN

Just like your food, furniture can be shipped miles to reach you. Cut down on your carbon footprint and support your local community by buying furniture from a local craftsman or employing a carpenter to make bespoke furniture for you. It doesn't always cost much more than mass-produced items.

105 VINTAGE IS GOOD VALUE

Pre-owned furniture can be the greenest option of all, and many vintage pieces have a charm and value that new items just don't have. Mid-century modern vintage, such as Eames chairs or Robin and Lucienne Day pieces, are also good investments as they have a high re-sale value. You can bid for them on eBay.

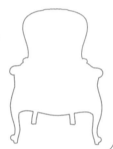

106 BE GREEN WITH GREENGUARD

Many furniture manufacturers such as Herman Miller, Haworth, Paoli and Knoll offer Greenguard certified furniture that is low-toxicity. The Greenguard programme provides ceritification of products based on their low-emissions.

107
SECOND-CYCLE FURNITURE

Many furniture designers are now using existing wood rather than new wood. Some comes from flawed wood or factory scraps while others are sourced from remnants from the logging industry. Artek, the manufacturer of Alvar Aalto chairs, has worked with British designer Tom Dixon to create a '2nd Cycle' line which rescues historic pieces, such as the Aalto Model No.60 chair, and resells them with information about that particular item's history (see www.artek.fi).

108
BUY CRADLE-TO-CRADLE

The cradle-to-cradle idea is that a product is endlessly recycleable – it never reaches a 'grave' or landfill at the end of it's useful life. Examples include office chairs from Herman Miller and Steelcase, but look for the C2C certification logo (see www.mbdc.com). Choose furniture that can easily be taken apart as this means the pieces can be recycled in other ways.

109

BE AWARE OF OFFGASSING

New non-metallic products that contain VOCs will 'offgas' for years, which means they will release chemicals into the surrounding air by evaporation (this is what you can identify as the 'new car smell') in your home or office. The effects are even more toxic in a well-insulated building. Buying second-hand furniture means that it has done most of its 'offgassing' already.

110

AN EFFICIENT MODEL

After central heating, fridges and freezers are the biggest domestic users of energy, because they're on all the time. Choose the most energy-efficient models – in the UK they will display the Energy Saving Recommended logo, in the EU buy only those that have achieved A+ or A++ on the EU Energy Label and in the US look for the Energy Star symbol.

111 THE RIGHT REFRIGERANT

You should insist on a fridge or freezer that uses a hydrocarbon (R600a) refrigerant and which is labelled 'CFC & HFC free'. Chlorofluorocarbons (CFCs) and HCFCs (hydrochlorofluorocarbons) are powerful greenhouse gases which are being phased out, while the HFCs (hydrofluorocarbons) that replaced them are also greenhouse gases – at least 1,200 times more powerful than CO_2 – so should be avoided. Greenpeace says that at expected rates of usage, by 2050 HFCs will contribute as much to global warming as all the private cars on the planet.

112 CHOOSE YOUR FREEZER WISELY

Freezers consume the most energy of all refrigeration products so opt for a chest freezer, rather than upright one, as they tend to be more energy efficient. Avoid frost-free freezers, which use on average 45% more energy than manually defrosted models. Look out too for 'dual control' fridge-freezers that allow you to turn the fridge off and leave the freezer on when you go away for longer.

113 PUTTING ON THE PRESSURE

Microwave ovens use 75% less energy than conventional ovens and don't produce surplus heat, while a pressure cooker can cook three or four times quicker than a conventional cooker, so both are good choices.

114 A QUICKER MORE EFFICIENT COOK

Induction hobs are more expensive than traditional hobs but consume half as much electricity as electric hobs and are more efficient in heat transfer. Manufacturers estimate that power savings of 40–70% are achievable in comparison to conventional hobs.

115

BUY A DECENT DISHWASHER

Research has found that dishwashers use only half the energy, one-sixth of the water and less soap than handwashing your dishes (provided they are used when full). Buy the most energy-efficient model possible as they can use up to 40% less energy than an inefficient appliance.

116

DRY WITH LAUNDRY BALLS

Drying balls have spikes on the outside to lift and separate clothing, allowing the heat and air in a tumble dryer to circulate more freely. Clothes dry more quickly and you use less energy. They also soften your laundry naturally by physically manipulating the fabric so you won't need to add chemical fabrics softeners. They can cut drying time by up to 25% and will last up to five years.

117 INVEST IN A DOUBLE FLUSH

Flushing the loo accounts for around 30% of total household water consumption and an old toilet can use as much as 9–12 litres (2½–3½ gallons) of water every time it's flushed. A good way to save water is to install a dual-flush model. These have one flush which uses around 2–3 litres (½–1 gallon) of water for liquid waste, and another, using 4–7 litres (1–2 gallons), for solids.

118 TAP INTO WATER TAPS

There are several devices available that reduce water use in your taps (faucets), one of which changes the water flow into a spray when you open the tap slightly. This will save on water use but can be over-ridden if you need to fill the basin quickly. Or you can fit flow regulators and limiting valves, which can be fitted into basins, baths and showers to control the water flow.

119 BUY A HIPPO!

A Hippo (www.hippo4life.co.uk) is a water displacement device that can save around 3 litres (1 gallon) of water every time you flush. It sits in your cistern and ensures that not all the water is used when flushed; therefore it won't take as much water to fill the cistern up either. You can achieve a similar saving by filling an old water bottle up and putting it in your cistern.

120 GREEN KITCHEN RE-MODELLING

There is a range of greener alternatives for kitchen countertops and units, including formaldehyde-free fiberboard made out of materials such as straw and wheat board. You can even buy countertops made from post-consumer recycled waste paper (such as Richlite).

121 AVOID ARTIFICIAL FRESHENERS

In Britain £300 million is spent each year on air fresheners and in the US 80% of households use 'home fragrances' regularly, but these chemical-heavy products have been linked to health problems. A US study of 14 air fresheners found that 12 of them contained chemicals linked to birth defects (phthalates), which were not listed as ingredients.

122 FRIENDLY DETERGENTS

A good choice of eco-friendly detergents are now available, the best of which you can buy in bulk or as refills. Look out too for concentrated detergents that you can either use sparingly or dilute yourself. These products are generally based on plant and natural mineral ingredients. They avoid phosphates, petroleum-based additives and chemicals such as optical brighteners, artificial enzymes and chlorine-based bleaches.

123

WASH WITH NUTS OR ECO BALLS

Give eco balls a whirl in your wash. They are reuseable for over 1,000 washes and soften clothes, too. Or try soapnuts – the fruit of the ritha tree found primarily in India and Nepal. The shell contains saponin, known for its ability to cleanse and wash, and they can be used in washing machines and dishwashers. After use, add them to your compost heap.

124

BUY AN E-CLOTH

E-cloths wipe away dirt, including grease, using just water. These micro-fibre cloths are sold for a variety of uses including cleaning kitchens and bathrooms, stainless steel, glass, mirrors, plastics, chrome, television and computer screens, car dashboards and wood. The cloth can also be boil-washed up to 300 times to ensure it isn't harbouring germs (although do this rarely to avoid wasting energy on a hot wash).

125 GREEN CLEANING KIT

Just a few core natural products can be combined to clean many areas around your home. To clean bathroom and kitchen surfaces, mix one cup of vinegar and one cup of water – the vinegar dissolves dirt, soap scum and hard water deposits. For the toilet bowl and showerhead, undiluted white vinegar will tackle both jobs: leave the showerhead in a bowl of it for at least two hours. For slow-running drains, pour half a cup of baking soda into the drain, wash down with a little hot water and leave overnight before rinsing thoroughly with hot water.

126 DON'T WASTE YOUR WASTE

A compost bin is one of the greenest things you can buy. It will provide a great home for your uncooked fruit and vegetables, lawn clippings and most other garden waste, egg shells, tea bags and coffee filters, newspaper and cardboard, old cut flowers and so on. Plus, you get a great product for your garden once it's all broken down naturally.

127 DON'T BUY PESTICIDES AND HERBICIDES

The British public spends around £50 million each year on pesticides such as slug pellets and weed killers, and American homeowners apply at least 90 million pounds of pesticides to their lawns and gardens annually. These chemicals endanger wildlife and could be putting you and your family's health at risk. A recent study, for example, has found a clear link between two commonly used weed killers and birth defects in children. There are many natural alternatives available.

128 BE THE BUTT

Another essential item for households, a water butt will make the most of the heavy downpours predicted as a result of climate change and could save the day in the long hot summers that are also on their way. Look out for an environmentally friendly butt made from recycled plastic.

GO GREY

A grey-water siphon pump is a simple device that allows you to use the water from your bath to water the garden. Just connect one end to your hosepipe and put the other in the bath. Natural atmospheric pressure will deliver the water to your garden, fill your water butt or help you wash the car.

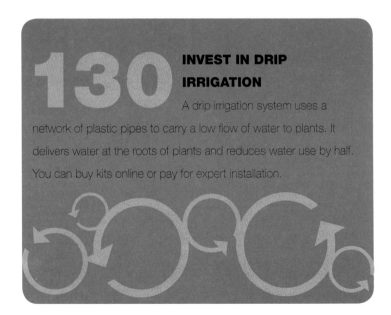

INVEST IN DRIP IRRIGATION

A drip irrigation system uses a network of plastic pipes to carry a low flow of water to plants. It delivers water at the roots of plants and reduces water use by half. You can buy kits online or pay for expert installation.

131 **BUY ORGANIC SEED**
Open-pollinated, locally adapted traditional seeds will ensure you are doing your bit to keep as many varieties of plants available and avoid the possible perils of genetic modification. Go for organic wherever possible.

132 **NON-WILD PLANTS AND BULBS**
While it is great to plant native species, it is vital that any wild plants and bulbs have not been collected from the wild. These plants are already under threat from introduced invasive species, habitat loss and climate change – they don't need to be uprooted and sold to gardeners as well. The practice will only stop if we don't buy them.

133

DON'T BUY POWER MOWERS

Petrol mowers produce more CO_2 than electric versions and are said to account for at least 5% of North America's air pollution – 54 million Americans mow their lawns each weekend with petrol-powered mowers. Buy a push mower instead – it gives you all the benefits of exercise without adding to carbon emissions. Or if your lawn is big, consider buying a solar-powered 'auto mower'.

134

OUTDOOR FURNISHING

A range of synthetic wood products is now available for outdoor furniture, fences and trellising. Made from recycled plastic and polystyrene, they are maintenance-free and can be used in fencing or elsewhere in your garden. Check the amount of recycled material used in the product before you buy.

135 USE AN ORGANIC PRESERVATIVE

There is an alternative to toxic, synthetic preservatives. For fence panels that are not in contact with the soil, apply linseed oil or similar products that allow the wood to breathe. Boron-based timber preservatives are also acceptable in organic gardening as they are safe for people and the environment.

136 AVOID TROPICAL HARDWOODS

The UK is the main importer of tropical hardwood furniture in Europe but a lot of it has come from unsustainable forests. Look out instead for alternatives, such as furniture made from recycled aluminium, reclaimed scaffold boards, cable drums and recycled tyres.

137

A STONE'S SOURCE

Imports of natural stone accounts for around 10% of the UK market for home paving and is expected to account for 20% within 10 years, but Indian sandstone is often being mined by very young children, working long hours in inhumane conditions. Many stone quarries in China are no better. Seek a supplier who can prove its stone is ethically sourced or, find your stone at reclamation yard or ask if there is any you can use locally at municipal waste recovery centres.

138

LIMIT THE LIMESTONE IN YOUR ROCKERY

Demand for limestone pavement stone for use in garden rockeries is leading to the devastation of naturally occurring limestone pavements and the special plants that live in them. Large amounts of illegally obtained pavement stone is being sold so wherever possible use reclaimed stone or buy moulded resin rocks which have been cast to look like pieces of limestone pavement.

139 GREEN DRIVEWAYS

Instead of a traditional paved driveway, use a permeable or 'pervious' asphault that incorporates void spaces. This type looks the same but allows more rainwater into the ground. This will reduce the burden on storm sewers and help remove pollutants. A grass paving system is also a good green option.

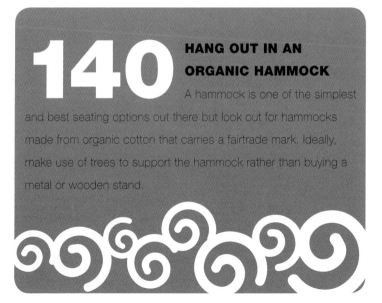

140 HANG OUT IN AN ORGANIC HAMMOCK

A hammock is one of the simplest and best seating options out there but look out for hammocks made from organic cotton that carries a fairtrade mark. Ideally, make use of trees to support the hammock rather than buying a metal or wooden stand.

141
SOLAR POWER IN THE GARDEN

There are a lot of solar-powered products for garden use including water features such as fountains, pond oxygenators, floating lights and security lights.

142
BUILD A BETTER BARBECUE

Up to 90% of the 40,000 tonnes of charcoal burnt in the UK each year is sourced from abroad, often from vulnerable tropical forests and mangrove swamps. There is enough woodland near most of us to be able to supply local charcoal and reduce transport pollution. Look for local, sustainable suppliers that carry the Forest Stewardship Council (FSC) logo.

143 AVOID BRIQUETTES

In the US, 63% of barbecues are fired with briquettes, consisting of waste timber and sawdust that is mixed with cornstarch to bind and a hydrocarbon solvent, similar to lighter fluid, to make them start easily. But according to the US Environmental Protection Agency, charcoal briquettes release 105 times more carbon monoxide per unit of energy than propane and a lot of toxic volatile organic compounds (VOCs).

144 DITCH THE DISPOSABLE

Disposable barbeques are a complete waste of resources and they cannot be recycled or composted. For a longer-lasting alternative buy a bucket barbeque – a galvanized bucket with air holes in the sides and bottom, a wooden handle and removable grill top.

145 PICNIC THE GREEN WAY

For a green picnic, buy picnic blankets made from 'shoddy' wool, which is the wool left over from the production of virgin wool blankets and biodegradeable picnic sets made from sustainable bamboo husk, which can be composted.

146 BE PREPARED TO PREPARE YOUR OWN

Give up ready-prepared meals. First there's the packaging – they usually come in plastic trays, covered with a plastic lid, and wrapped in cardboard – then there's the energy hungry process of cooking, chilling and possibly freezing, before cooking again. Beyond their dubious contribution to your health, prepared meals really are no good for the planet.

147 BUY LESS FOOD

Many households in prosperous countries buy more than they actually need. Recent research has shown that a third of food bought in the UK is thrown away and that 90% of customers are completely unaware of the amount of food they've disposed of. Most of this waste food ends up in landfill, where it produces the greenhouse gas methane.

148 KEEP IT SEASONAL

If you eat local food that is readily available in a particular season you'll be saving money and reducing the demand for imported food. You'll also really appreciate those first strawberries of summer if you stop buying the imported ones throughout winter.

149 LOOK FOR LESS PACKAGING

A recent survey has found that 40% of the packaging in the average UK shopping basket has to be buried because it is not recyclable, and about one-third of America's trash is made up of packaging, with about 10 cents of every dollar spent paying for the packaging. There is an increasing number of recycled and biodegradeable wrapping and bagging options now available. Or buy products that have no packaging at all.

150 BUY ORGANIC FOOD

Want to cut back on the pesticides in your diet? Then be sure to buy organic food. Up to 40% of the fruit, vegetable and bread samples tested in the UK were found to contain pesticides; while in the US, consumers can experience up to 70 daily exposures to residues through their diets. Even worse, government tests have found that 70% of samples of free school fruit and vegetables given to children in the UK contained pesticide residues and 1.7% had residues above the legally permitted limits.

151 BEWARE CHEAP PRAWNS (SHRIMP)

Annual sales of prawns (shrimp) are growing at an average of 9% a year but this demand is driving environmental destruction around the world. Nearly 40% of world mangrove loss has been attributed to shrimp farming, and mangroves are among the most productive ecosystems on the planet. Madagascar is working towards making all its prawn fisheries sustainable so if you do buy them, look out for organic or Madagascan varieties.

152 PICK FAIRTRADE COFFEE

Tea and coffee are grown solely in developing countries, mainly in areas of outstanding natural beauty where biodiversity is dependent upon environmentally sensitive farming. So it is vital that you support the greenest possible brands by buying organic and fairtrade tea and coffee.

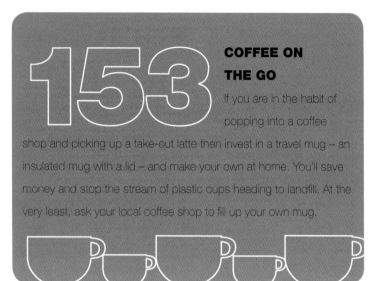

153

COFFEE ON THE GO

If you are in the habit of popping into a coffee shop and picking up a take-out latte then invest in a travel mug – an insulated mug with a lid – and make your own at home. You'll save money and stop the stream of plastic cups heading to landfill. At the very least, ask your local coffee shop to fill up your own mug.

154

SUPPORT YOUR MILKMAN

If you are lucky enough to live in an area with a milk delivery service, then add your name to the milkman's list. They generally supply milk from local farms and will take your empty bottles and reuse them. A glass milk bottle is typically reused between 9 and 40 times and then recycled.

155 BUY RECYCLED FOIL

Producing aluminium (aluminum) foil is an energy-intensive process so you should avoid using it if at all possible. For those times when nothing else will do make sure you buy foil made from 100% recycled aluminium – it takes 95% less energy to produce recycled foil. And remember, it can be recycled many times, so give it a wipe and reuse it.

156 NATURALLY CORKED

Pick a wine that is sealed with natural cork rather than the plastic variety or a metal screw top. Natural cork comes from the world's relatively small population of cork oak trees, mostly found in Portugal and Spain. The survival of these forests, which according to the WWF rank among the top biodiversity hotspots in the Mediterranean and in Europe, relies on the continued demad for cork. Important species such as the Iberian lynx, the Barbary deer and the black stork depend on these forests for their survival.

157 BUY ORGANIC, NON-GM

Nearly all the milk, dairy products and pork in UK supermarkets comes from animals fed on genetically modified (GM) crops, and none of this is labelled, according to the organic certifier the Soil Association. It found that around 60% of the maize and 30% of the soya fed to dairy cattle and pigs is GM, so most people are unwittingly eating food produced from GM crops every day.

158 WATCH OUT FOR GMOS

GM crops have been engineered to be resistant to herbicides, to produce toxins to kill pests, or to provide higher yields. There are many questions about the possible environmental and health impact of genetically modified organisms (GMOs) but avoiding them can be tough. In the US, GM foods and products are currently not labelled and roughly 70% of the foods in supermarkets have GM ingredients. In the EU, products have to be labelled if they are from a GM source, but not if they have been produced with GM technology or come from animals fed on GM animal feed. Organic standards prohibit the use of GM ingredients or GM feed.

159 BUY LESS MEAT

The stomachs of the world's 1.4 billion cows account for 14% of global emissions of methane, a greenhouse gas 20 times more potent than CO_2. Plus, it takes far more energy, land and water to produce the equivalent amount of calories from meat than from grain or soya beans – it has been estimated that growing grains, vegetables and fruits uses only 5% as many raw materials as that used in meat production.

160 THE MSC LOGO

Over half of fish stocks are being fished at their maximum biological capacity and only 3% of the world's fish stocks are underexploited. But, over the last 30 years, demand for seafood products has doubled and is anticipated to grow at 1.5% per year through to 2020. One option is to look for the Marine Stewardship Council (MSC) logo that shows the product is from a well-managed and sustainable fishery.

GIVE A COD A BREAK

Cod stocks have plummeted and are on the verge of collapse in some areas; there is also a problem with illegally caught cod. Don't assume hake or hoki are sustainable alternatives to cod, as their stocks are also overexploited and they are mostly caught by bottom trawlers, which plough the seabed causing habitat destruction and catching corals, sharks and skates. Opt for pollack, saithe, blue whiting, herring and mackerel.

162 CERTIFIED FARMED FISH

Buy your fish from reputable suppliers and insist on fish from a sustainable source. There are bodies that certify fish farms – in the UK, the Soil Association certifies organically farmed salmon, while FRIEND of the Sea (FotS) in the US certifies and promotes seafood from sustainable fisheries and aquaculture including organically farmed cod and trout.

163 SIGN UP FOR A BOX

Find out if your area supports a local vegetable box programme that delivers seasonal fruit and vegetables to your door every week. Many of them stock a wide range of other ethical and organic products, too. Ideally pick one that uses produce from local suppliers.

164 BUY FROM FARMERS

Buying directly from farmers, at a farmer's market for example, helps support local producers and ensure that the goods you buy have not travelled miles to reach you. But do check that the suppliers really are local.

165 THINK THROUGH THE AIR MILES DEBATE

Dropping all air-freighted food from your shopping list might be a good idea for the planet but could be disastrous for fragile farming communities in the developing world. UK certifier the Soil Association may offer a possible solution to the dilemma – it is planning from January 2009 to only certify air-freighted organic food if it meets its own Ethical Trade standards or the Fairtrade Foundation's standards, and companies will have to develop plans for reducing any remaining dependence on air freight.

166 RAISE A GLASS TO ORGANIC BEER

Your regular beer could be made with hops that have been sprayed up to 14 times each year with an average of 15 pesticide products. Organic beer is made from organic malt and hops using farming methods that rule out this kind of chemical saturation.

167 GRAPE EXPECTATIONS

Avoid guzzling pesticide residues with your wine by buying organic. Around 17 pesticides are commonly used in non-organic vineyards, many of which are known irritants and suspected carcinogens, and residues of these chemicals have been found in wine. Less sulphur dioxide is added to certified organic wines – on average, organic producers use just one quarter of the legal maximum for conventional wines.

168 DRINK ORGANIC MILK

Several studies have shown that organic milk has higher levels of certain nutrients than non-organic milk, including omega-3, Vitamin E and beta-carotene. A recent study has also shown that the number of cases of eczema in children fed on organic dairy products, and whose mothers also consumed organic dairy products, are 36% lower than in children who consume conventional dairy products.

169   DON'T HELP THE SUPERBUGS

Most intensively reared farm animals are fed antibiotics on a daily basis, as growth promoters, as a preventative measure or to treat illness, but this use of antibiotics is thought to be linked to the onslaught of antibiotic-resistant superbugs such as MRSA. Antibiotics are permitted only very occasionally in organic farming and organic farmers have to wait a long time before meat, milk or eggs from treated animals can be sold for human consumption.

170   KEEP OFF THE BOTTLE

Bottled water is now the world's fastest-growing drinks sector. In the US, consumers purchased 28.4 billion litres (over 7 billion gallons) of bottled water in 2005, while in the UK half the population now drink over 2 billion litres (528 million gallons) of bottled water. The non-degradeable bottles are clogging up landfills and a huge amount of energy is used to make and transport them.

171 WHAT DOES YOUR WINE WEIGH?

Some retailers have started using lighter glass bottles for wines, which need less energy to transport. Other wines are packaged in cartons made from renewable materials, which are also a lighter load. Given that in most nations a large proportion of wines are imported, choosing the lightest possible packaging will help reduce your carbon footprint.

172 CRUSH YOUR CANS

A can-crusher is a simple wall-mounted device that reduces cans to about one-fifth of their original size – allowing your recycling collection service to fit more in their vehicle and reduce the number of trips they have to make. Aluminium cans and foils can be recycled endlessly and a new drinks' can could be back on the shelf in as little as 60 days after collection.

173 THE FLIGHT OF THE FLOWER

Avoid buying cut flowers unless you are certain of their origin. Flowers bought in supermarkets have often been airfreighted and refrigerated. There is also the issue of pesticides used in commercial flower production, which have an impact on the environment as well as the welfare of workers. UK consumers spend around £1.9 billion on cut flowers every year. The US is the second-largest importer worldwide – in 2006, cut flower imports totalled $768 million.

174 BUY ORGANIC COTTON

If you are keen to green your wardrobe start with organic cotton items. Cotton farming uses one-quarter of the world's pesticides and 20,000 deaths occur in developing countries each year from pesticide poisoning. According to the World Health Organisation, many of these can be attributed to cotton production.

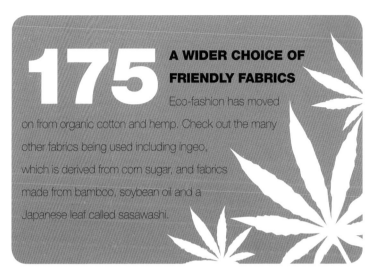

175 A WIDER CHOICE OF FRIENDLY FABRICS

Eco-fashion has moved on from organic cotton and hemp. Check out the many other fabrics being used including ingeo, which is derived from corn sugar, and fabrics made from bamboo, soybean oil and a Japanese leaf called sasawashi.

176 PLASTIC TEXTILES

Look out for recycled plastic bottles. The company Patagonia, which has used recycled soda bottles to create fleeces for many years through their Common Threads programme, claims it has now kept 86 million soda bottles out of landfills. They also give you background on their products – where the materials were sourced and the manufacturing processes involved.

177 THE WHOLE PROCESS

Eco-friendly fashion doesn't just rest on the type of fabric used. There are now entire clothing and accessory lines devoted to sustainable production practices – using wind power to provide the necessary energy for manufacture, using only organic fibres, and donating profits back to earth-friendly causes. For example, Prana, which designs and distributes yoga and climbing gear, supports wind farms and now supplies wind power to 400 retailers worldwide.

178 START SWISHING!

Swishing is essentially a clothes swap with a party atmosphere. Attendees arrive with at least one good quality item of clothing or an accessory and leave with a new outfit, having successfully recycled their unwanted clothes without having spent any money (www.swishing.org). If there isn't one in your area, be the first and organize a swishing party with your friends.

179 REMADE CLOTHES

Check out companies that take discarded clothes, give them a refurb and sell them on. TRAID (Textile Recycling for Aid and International Development) in the UK, for example, operates textile recycling banks, then repairs and customizes items before selling them. In this way they raise funds for overseas development and environmental projects.

180 SHAWL WARNING

Never buy Shahtoosh shawls – they are woven from the hair of the Tibetan antelope, which is killed in the process. Due to poaching, the Tibetan antelope is an endangered species. Look out for alternatives including nettle shawls (yes, woven from the plant), hemp shawls or a wool pashmina.

181 DON'T DRY-CLEAN

Despite its name, dry-cleaning is not totally dry. It involves the use of solvents that remove most stains, and most drycleaners use perchloroethylene, or PERC, as their main solvent. In high levels, PERC has been shown to cause cancer and its release into the air, ground and water is an environmental concern. There are greener alternatives offered by some cleaners but the best solution is to buy clothes that you can wash at low temperatures every now and then.

182 THE GREENEST CLOTHING...

... is already owned – by you! Look at mending and repairing existing clothes, having a tailor take them in or let them out, or otherwise re-structure them so you can get more mileage without further outlay of cost or manufacturing. If your clothing is completely beyond repair, cut them up to use in a patchwork quilt or as household rags. Get into the habit of reusing items until they can't be reused any longer.

183 BUY QUALITY CLOTHES

Don't be tempted by bargain-basement clothing stores and the idea of wearing today and throwing away tomorrow – this is ecologically unsound. Instead, buy better-quality items that may cost more but last many years. They will be made from good fibres so can be recycled and reused, and will be closer to natural sources than cheaper manmade alternatives.

184 WASH CLOTHING LESS

Even the most eco-friendly garment, such as an organic cotton T-shirt, can be costly in green terms due to the frequency it needs to be washed. Try to get several uses out of a garment before washing it, and sponge off small stains and marks rather than washing the entire garment.

185 CHOOSE REPUTABLE GREEN BRANDS

Fashion retailers such as People Tree (www.peopletree.co.uk), Edun (www.edunonline.com) and Loomstate (www.loomstate. org) are established as having good green credentials but are also able to keep up with every current trend. Their clothing has been spotted on celebrities and the catwalk.

186 LOOK FOR LOCAL MANUFACTURERS AND DESIGNERS

Socially responsible fashion retailers such as American Apparel have made good use of keeping all the processes close to home – in this case, materials, design and manufacturing are all based in Los Angeles. Obviously, the green idea gets diluted the further afield the brand sells, so take matters into your own hands and find a local solution. Something as simple as employing a neighbour to make beautiful knitwear for you can help the cause.

187

HOW WAS IT MADE?

The average manufacturing wage in China is 64 US cents an hour, according to the US Bureau of Labor Statistics, and wages in Mexico and Indonesia are similarly low. Avoid buying products from manufacturers known to use sweatshops and write to these companies telling them you won't give them your business because of their labour record.

188

CHAIN OF COMMAND

It is often impossible to track the history of your product because there can be as many as nine different subcontractors involved in one clothing item, from fibre to packaging, with unfair labour practices employed anywhere down the line. But the more questions you ask, the more companies will acknowledge the need for them to be accountable. Ask where the materials are sourced and where the manufacturing takes place and under what labour conditions.

189 CHECK YOUR LABEL

If the garment you are buying has a label naming a country or organization that you suspect employs unfair labour, find out more before you buy. Any developing country should automatically be considered of potential concern.

190 FRIENDLY FOOTWEAR

There are a growing number of eco-friendly shoe options out there, such as those from clothing company Patagonia who use leather uppers from tanneries that comply with ISO 14001 (a strict set of environmental standards), outsoles made from up to 30% recycled scrap rubber, and latex outsoles or midsoles made from the milk of the hevea tree.

191 REUSE A SHOE

Support companies which offer recycling options such as Nike's 'Reuse-A-Shoe' programme, which collects old trainers and turns them into 'Nike grind' – a material used to make play grounds and sports' surfaces.

192 RECYCLED AND FAIRTRADE SPORTSWEAR

When shopping for trainers (sneakers), consider those with ethics in mind. Several companies are manufacturing styles that are totally green but also have street-cool good looks, such as Worn Again (www.wornagain.co.uk), Green Toe by Simple (www.simpleshoes.com/greentoe) and Ethletic (www.ethletic.com).

193 LEATHER-FREE SHOES

If you are concerned about animal rights and the use of leather in your shoes, choose leather-free and animal-derivative-free alternatives. You don't need to sacrifice style for ethics. Fashionistas can do no better than buying Stella McCartney styles, but Beyond Skin (www.beyondskin.co.uk) and Moo Shoes (www. mooshoes.com) are also good alternatives.

194 ECO HANDBAGS AND ACCESSORIES

There are now many retailers that use recycled or discarded goods for handbags, totes and other fashion items. Ecoist (www.ecoist.com) uses discontinued or defectively printed snack wrappers to create stylish clutches, coin purses, bags and totes, while other companies such as Passchal (www.passchal.com) use tyre rubber to construct new items.

195 SECOND-HAND DIAMONDS

If you're in the market for a diamond, buy an antique rather than support the diamond industry, which has a poor environmental and human rights record. Conflict diamonds (also known as blood diamonds) are diamonds mined and traded illegally to help fund wars in Africa. Although a certification scheme – the Kimberley Process – has been set up, they are still being smuggled.

196 GOLD ETHICS

In the UK alone, nearly 20 million hallmarked gold articles are sold each year – equivalent to around a third of the population – but for every gold ring made, 18 tonnes of waste is produced, including cyanide and arsenic, and a large gold mine will draw around 830 litres (220 gallons) of water per minute. It is also estimated that between 1995 and 2015, roughly half the world's gold will have come from indigenous people's lands – much of it without those communities' consent. Look instead for ethically sourced gold.

197

BUY RECYCLED JEWELLERY

Forget about conventional gold and diamonds and buy jewellery made from recycled materials. The choice is huge, with jewellery made from recycled plastic bags and old shampoo bottles, recycled glass, old buttons, cutlery and more.

198

PICK YOUR PAPER WISELY

The average British person uses over 100 rolls of toilet paper per year. Look out for products marked as 100% recycled and unbleached. Products carrying the FSC Recycled logo are guaranteed to contain only post-consumer waste material. The next best choice is toilet roll with a high-recycled content or products carrying the FSC Mixed Sources label, which guarantees that the product is a mixture of fibres from an FSC-certified forest or a controlled source, or post-consumer reclaimed material.

199 SMILE GREEN

Just think how many plastic toothbrushes you'll get through in a lifetime and you'll see the point in buying 100% recycled and recyclable plastic toothbrushes. Find them online and buy some natural toothpaste at the same time – these use natural herbs, oils and minerals to clean your teeth rather than detergents, sodium lauryl sulphate, saccharine, artificial colours, synthetic preservatives or chemical whiteners.

200 NATURAL OR NOT?

The beauty sector seems to be more liberal with the truth on labels than most others. Be sceptical about any products that claim to be organic, natural or pure – words that can be used without any evidence to support them. It's best to buy organically certified products. In the US, organic bodycare products will display the USDA certified organic symbol, while in the UK, the Soil Association certifies bodycare products and is working with a group of EU certification bodies to develop a common European organic beauty and cosmetic standard.

201 BEAUTY CHEMICAL-FREE

According to the Environmental Working Group, nearly 90% of ingredients in US personal care products have not been assessed for safety by anyone and nearly 400 products sold in the US contain chemicals that are not allowed in other countries. Although in Europe the situation is slightly better due to new laws which will ban certain chemicals, it is still best to buy the least chemical-laden beauty products you can.

202 NATURAL NAILS

Nail varnishes, glues and other nail products can contain a cocktail of chemicals such as formaldehyde and tolulene – known carcinogens. A study has shown that 89% of the 10,000 chemicals used in nail-care products in the US have not been safety tested by an independent agency. Look out for more natural nail products that do not contain phthalates, toxins, formaldehyde, toluene or colour lakes (colour bases that do not break down in nature) and are preservative-free.

203 GO SKIN DEEPER

You can find safety information on specific products online by checking the Skin Deep database of nearly 25,000 bodycare products (www.cosmeticsdatabase.com). It will also tell you if a company has signed the Compact for Safe Cosmetics, whereby they pledge not to use chemicals linked to cancer, birth defects or mutation and to replace them with safer alternatives within three years.

204 LIP SERVICE

The average lipstick-wearing woman is thought to ingest the equivalent of 1 kg (2¼ lb) of lipstick over the course of their lives, so the ingredients matter. A recent report has found that commonly used lipstick manufactured in the US contains surprisingly high levels of lead – a neurotoxin – and one third of those brands containing lead exceeded the US Food and Drug Administration's limit for lead in sweets. Opt for natural brands and quiz every company on what they actually use in their products, not just what they list.

205

KIT OUT YOUR KID FOR SCHOOL

Give your children an eco-friendly school starter kit and look online for the following: lunchboxes made from recycled juice packs, fairtrade and organic cotton uniforms, school bags made from recycled plastic bottles, pens made from recycled car parts, pencil cases made from recycled car tyres and pencils made from CD cases and plastic cups. Top it all off with a water-powered calculator.

206

THE NAPPY (DIAPER) MOUNTAIN

Disposable nappy (diaper) waste is the third largest source of solid waste in the US, where some 18 billion nappies are thrown away every year, while in the UK nearly 3 billion are binned each year – 90% of which end up in landfill and take years to decompose. Avoid adding to the waste mountain by buying real nappies, ideally made from organic cotton and hemp and worn with organic wool waterproof overpants.

207 GIVE A GREEN PARTY

Ditch the plastic party bags with cheap plastic toys that are thrown away after each party. Instead buy brown paper bags, which your children can decorate, and include a slice of cake along with some useful non-plastic items such as paint brushes, crayons or books. Or use an eco-friendly and ethical party bag supplier that offers recycled or reusable bags filled with fairtrade chocolate and recycled gifts.

208 WOODEN TOYS

Say no to plastic battery-operated toys and instead look for toys made from sustainably sourced wood. It is estimated that up to 80% of toys in US stores have been made in China, but wouldn't it be great if more of us bought our toys from local manufacturers to avoid the energy and emission costs of transportation?

209 LUNCHBOX CHOICES

Food manufacturers are coming up with increasing amounts of lunchbox products that are usually among the worst offenders in terms of wasteful packaging. Avoid the separately packaged biscuits (crackers), cheeses and yogurts and instead buy in bulk and use reusable pots to provide snack-size portions.

210 KEEP YOUR KIDS CHEMICAL-FREE

Avoid conventional, processed food if you want to have a calm family life. A recent study by the UK's Food Standards Agency has found that children behaved impulsively and lost concentration after consuming a drink containing additives and certain mixtures of artificial-food colours, along with sodium benzoate (E211) – a preservative used in ice cream and confectionery. Most of the 290 additives allowed are prohibited in organic foods, including all artificial colours or flavourings.

211 BABY BOTTLE WARNING

A recent US study has found a toxic chemical called bisphenol A, which is linked to developmental, neural and reproductive problems, leaches into liquids and foods from commonly used clear plastic baby bottles. The US Center for Disease Control and Prevention found bisphenol A in the urine of over 95% of people they tested. It's best to either buy glass bottles or check with the manufacturer whether the bottle contains the chemical.

212 BUY RECYCLED LITTER

The litter from America's 90 million pet cats results in around two millions tonnes of cat litter being sent to landfills each year. To reduce the environmental impact, avoid the clay-based varieties of pet litters, which don't biodegrade and are often dusted with silica, a known carcinogen that can cause respiratory disease. Choose a litter made from recycled material such as sawmill scrap or waste from wheat or corn.

213 POOP DISPOSAL

Removing your pets' faeces from public areas is an environmental must – America's 73 million dogs produce around 10 million tonnes of dog poop per year – but be sure it goes in a biodegradeable bag so all of it breaks down once disposed of.

214 TREAT PETS NATURALLY

Flea powders and worm tablets are just some of the chemical nasties we buy for our pets, but they are dangerous to have in the home and could end up polluting the environment when disposed of. There are plenty of natural alternatives, such as homeopathic remedies, that are worth a try.

215 DITCH THE PACKAGING

Pet food should be bought in bulk to avoid throwing away huge amounts of packaging. Avoid food that is sold in individual sachets for each meal and look out for compostable or biodegradeable packaging.

216 BUY LESS AT CHRISTMAS

This is the one time of the year when even the most eco-friendly among us seem to be lured into a consumer frenzy, but it is incredibly wasteful. In the UK alone, people get through 83 sq km (32 sq miles) of wrapping paper, a billion Christmas cards, plus 125,000 tonnes of plastic packaging, and nearly 3,000 tonnes of aluminium foil from the turkey. Buy less of everything at Christmas and you can feel virtuous as well as festive!

217

LESS OF THE TWINKLE

Each Christmas sees increasing numbers of homes decked with hundreds of twinkling lights. It has been estimated that decorating your whole house with lights indoors and out could use up 1,000 kWh of electricity – almost a third of the annual electricity used by an average home.

218

DECK THE HALLS WITH BOUGHS OF GREEN

In 2006, the UK imported 60,000 tonnes of Christmas decorations from China most of which was discarded at the end of the festive season. There are so many greener ways of decorating your home – collect and paint some pine cones or fallen branches, make gingerbread tree decorations instead of using plastic baubles, get the children to make paper chains etc. Failing that, several websites now offer eco-friendly decorations that should last and last.

219

LOOK INTO LEDS

For lighting up your tree this Christmas, consider using LED (light emitting diodes) lighting. They use a fraction of the energy of a conventional bulb (estimates say around 10% of the power used by conventional fairly lights). LED lights are expensive but remember 'less is more' when it comes to Christmas decor.

220

BE GREEN WITH GIFTS

From adopting an endangered animal (through the WWF) to a solar-powered toy car, the scope for green gifts is enormous. There are hundreds of green gift stores online so there's no excuse for that pile of plastic under your tree on Christmas morning.

221 WRAP WITH CARE

Don't forget to wrap your green gifts carefully – choose 100% post-consumer recycled paper or pick a hand-made and hand-printed, fairly traded gift wrap. Instead of using sticky tape, use either ribbons, string or wool – they can be re-used and make the paper easier to reuse. Avoid bubble wrap or polystyrene packing material for delicate items and instead use old newspaper to cushion fragile items.

222 TAKE CARE WITH GREETINGS CARDS

When shopping for greetings cards look for 100% post-consumer waste content and processed chlorine-free (PCF) paper products, where no additional chlorine or chlorine derivatives were used to bleach the final recycled-fibre product. Better still make your own or send digital cards online. Remember also to recycle your cards.

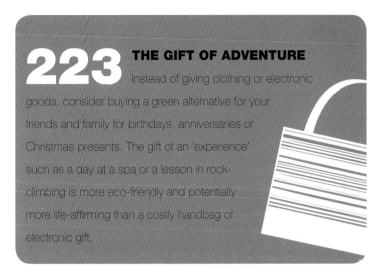

223 THE GIFT OF ADVENTURE

Instead of giving clothing or electronic goods, consider buying a green alternative for your friends and family for birthdays, anniversaries or Christmas presents. The gift of an 'experience' such as a day at a spa or a lesson in rock-climbing is more eco-friendly and potentially more life-affirming than a costly handbag or electronic gift.

224 CHARITY-GIVING GIFT

Consider a gift of charity for a present – this is usually something people want to do but don't get around to, so do it for them! Whether it's giving money for a specific environmental cause (see www.oneclickatatime.org), buying laptops for children (One Laptop Per Child, www.laptopgiving.org) or a product from any number of charity websites, such as the WWF, it makes a thoughtful gift.

225 HAIL A GREEN CAB

They are on the road night and day, so imagine the benefits if cabs were to go green. Well, some taxi operators are now offering 'greener' services by using greener cars. In London, there are already several services to choose from, most of which use Toyota Prius cars which they claim emit 60% less CO_2 than standard taxis.

226 INVEST IN A GREENER CAR

Those featured at the top of the Environmental Transport Association list are the Honda Civic 1.4 IMA Executive, a petrol/electric hybrid, and the Toyota Prius 1.5 Hybrid – the most efficient mass-produced car on the market with the lowest CO_2 emissions of all cars.

227

GET GOOD TYRES

There are over three billion discarded car tyres in the US, with over 200 million more added each year. They pollute landfills, present a fire hazard and waste oil. When you shop for tyres, look for the longest-wearing tyres you can find and keep them properly inflated to reduce wear and save fuel. Retreading saves about 1.5 billion litres (400 million gallons) of oil each year.

228

ON TWO WHEELS

In the UK, 6.6 million people travel less than five miles to work, so if they all travelled there by bike it would save 44 million tonnes of CO_2 – equivalent to the emissions from heating more than 16,000 homes for a year. While in the US only 0.4% of commuters use a bicycle.

229 GREEN CYCLE STORAGE

If storing your bike is a problem then Cycloc could be the answer. Made from 100% recycled plastic, Cycloc fixes to the wall and allows you to store your bike above the floor, which means you can win back your hallway, or make space in your garage.

230 ELECTRIC MOTORING

Consider buying an electric car. With absolutely no emissions, these are a great solution to our society's reliance on petrol (gas). Although hampered by low speeds, they are excellent alternatives for city-users and small commutes. Battery-cell versions simply plug into an electric outlet. Alternatively, choose a hybrid vehicle, which uses a combination of battery and petrol – the battery is used for slower speeds with petrol only kicking in for the higher mph.

231 DON'T BUY A CAR, USE A CAB

If you are an urban dweller, think carefully about buying a car. Taxis, which are already on the road, are a service that's used by others when they're not being used by you. Look out for hybrid vehicles or pedi-cabs and cycle rickshaws.

232 SHARE IN A CAR RENTAL SCHEME

There are now car-sharing schemes operating in many major cities. These allow you to book a car online, pick it up around the corner and drop it back into a designated bay on a pay-per-hour basis. It has all the benefits of owning a car but without the hassle.

233 THE ENV MOTORBIKE

Motorbikes emit 16 times the amount of hydrocarbons, including greenhouse gases, compared to cars, but innovation is on the way with the Emissions Neutral Vehicle (ENV) fuel-cell motorbike by Seymour Powell. It has a top speed of 80 kmh (50 mph) and can run for four hours before the fuel cell needs recharging.

234 SAVE FARES AND TIME

Learn to love public transportation by searching out cheap weekly or off-peak tickets which will encourage you to use the service. In addition, buses, trains, light rail and ferries have dedicated travel routes that are usually much faster than car travel.

235 PORTABLE BIKES

There are several lightweight folding bikes on the market, such as the Strida and GoBike, which make daily cycling so much easier and convenient. The advantage is that you can cycle even as part of a longer commute by public transportation, because the bikes are easy to fold up and carry. At an average speed of 15–20 kph (10–12 mph), they are fast, green and cheap.

236 NO NEED FOR FOUR-WHEEL DRIVE

One of the biggest green 'crimes' is buying a larger version of a product than you actually need, and this really applies to four-wheel drives. Most people who drive them never take them off the highway. Not only are they petrol (gas) guzzling polluters, but they aren't even being used for their purpose. Environmental issues aside, before buying one consider whether you will actually use this car for the purpose for which it's intended.

237

REDUCE AIR TRAVEL

A single flight across country in the US produces about 10% as much carbon as the total of everything else that the average American does in a year. If you can replace a jet trip with a train ride, it will reduce carbon dioxide emissions by 85–96%.

238

OFFSET YOUR MILES

Carbon offsetting is a way of neutralizing the carbon emissions you emit when you drive or fly. You subscribe to an offsetting organization and donate money every time you travel – these funds then go towards planting trees and installing solar panels and wind turbines. Some airlines are now routinely asking for offsetting donations when people book their trips.

239

STOP FLYING

Aviation accounts for just over 3.5% of total CO_2 emissions worldwide and the Intergovernmental Panel on Climate Change estimates that by 2050 emissions from aircraft could be responsible for up to 15% of total global warming produced by human activities. Aviation emissions are estimated to have between two and four times the climate change impact of carbon emissions alone.

240

POST-CONSUMER READING

Buy only books or magazines that have been printed on recycled paper. Paper production accounts for about 43% of harvested wood and recycling of newsprint saves about 1 tonne of wood. It is also estimated that recycling one tonne of newspaper saves about 4,000 kWh of electricity – enough electricity to power a three-bedroom European house for a year, or to heat and air-condition the average North American home for almost six months.

241

ECO-FRIENDLY BREAKS

Holidays don't have to mean a highly polluting flight to a resort in a hot and usually water-stressed part of the world. Choose from a huge variety of eco-friendly holidays, preferably close to home, such as a boating holiday on a UK canal, with a percentage of the booking cost donated to the Waterways Trust Green Fund.

242

THREATENED SPECIES

What seems like a good souvenir purchase at the time could be costing the planet dear and land you in prison. Products to watch out for are those made with ivory, coral and turtle-shell products – six of the seven species of marine turtles are endangered or critically endangered and all international trade in marine turtle products is banned. Find out if you need a CITES (the Convention on International Trade in Endangered Species of Wild Fauna and Flora) permit to bring it home from your travels.

243 SUSTAINABLE SOUVENIRS

The campaign group Common Ground is campaigning for producers and those working in tourism to provide locally distinctive souvenirs that are made nearby, from local renewable materials, demonstrating sustainable production and that are ethically derived, fairly traded and offering fair value (www.commonground.org.uk).

244 SAVE IT FOR THE SHORT HAUL

Instead of taking exotic long-haul journeys abroad, look close to home for your holidays and breaks to cut down on your air miles. If you can't go by train or bus, even a short flight is more eco-friendly than one that takes you halfway around the world for a change of scenery you can get in a two-hour flight.

245 MAKE YOUR TRIP COUNT

Check out volunteering breaks so that during part or all of your vacation you can contribute to bettering the local environment, whether it's cleaning beaches or planting crops.

246 GREEN COFFIN OPTIONS

This may be one shopping trip you won't be on, but you can specify in advance what your choice would be! Consider asking for a green coffin. They can be made in bamboo, wicker, willow or cardboard and are biodegradeable and made from sustainable sources – some even carry a fairtrade mark.

247 ETHICAL INVESTMENTS

You may not see your financial agreements as part of your weekly shop, but they are and they could be green. Your bank or investment fund may put your money into the oil or GM-food business. Move your money to a bank, or insurance company that supports environmentally and ethically sound businesses.

248 ECO-FRIENDLY CREDIT

There's even a green store card for you card junkies out there. CarbonCred lets shoppers earn green points at high-street stores and the virtual card is accepted at 1,000 online stores. The reward points you notch up can then be spent on carbon-busting products and services (www.CarbonCred.co.uk). Many credit card companies in the US now offer eco-friendly choices for its reward-card holders – for such options as donating to a renewable-energy cause.

249 DON'T HEAT YOUR PATIO

Over 600,000 gas-powered heaters adorn the patios and decking areas of UK households, adding in excess of 350,000 tonnes of additional CO_2 to the atmosphere every year. Our advice? Just put on a jacket.

250 INSURANCE WEATHER WATCH

The increase in extreme weather conditions around the world has prompted some insurance companies to look at the causes and effects of climate change, in order to re-evaluate calculations which were traditionally based on past findings. Ask your insurer how climate change effects, such as increased risk of flooding and storms, will affect your cover.